101
BEST
JEWISH JOKES

Narrated,

occasionally

commented on,

also with an

introduction (short)

by

Hershel Shanks

Illustrations by Dave Clark

MOMENT Publications
Washington, D.C.

INTRODUCTION

Despite the numbering system from 1 to 101, are there really 101 jokes in this book? Some will find more. But others will find fewer; they'll say some are not really jokes.

Are they all jokes? Or are some just insightful comments? (And sometimes not so insightful?)

Perhaps more important: Are they all Jewish? What makes a Jewish joke anyway? So why the title?

And are these the best? As you read these jokes, many of you will immediately think of a better one. Or a different version that is better. Obviously, no two people would make the same 101 choices.

Above all, are they funny? The answer to this question will, in almost each case, vary widely from person to person and from joke to joke, especially regarding jokes that depend on the telling—the timing, the inflection, the accent. It is much easier to be funny orally than in writing. It will also depend on just what interests you Jewishly. I've noticed this in telling these jokes. There may also be a difference in generations. What's funny to one generation is not to their children. Or vice versa. Do you like word plays? Are you deeply involved in tradition? Do you speak Yiddish? If you're not interested in the subject, making fun of it or making a joke about it won't amuse you.

Then, there is the question of taste, in the sense of, "Are some of these jokes tasteless?" There are a few jokes here that you may find tasteless.

Some depend on Jewish stereotypes. Some don't reflect well on Jews. Sometimes it's OK when Jews tell these jokes among Jews, but not OK if non-Jews tell them. Some reflect prejudice against non-Jews. But they are never mean, only stereotypical.

All I can say is that I hope you will find the contents for the most part enjoyable and that the book will be difficult to put down, a little like a bag of potato chips—*just one more.*

Many books have been written about Jewish humor but they never really seem to pin it down—neither Jewish, nor humor. So I won't try. Just let it flow—but I'd be glad to hear from you.

The jokes in this book are not just thrown together haphazardly. They are roughly divided by type, for example, jokes that depend on a double entendre or jokes about Israel or jokes about Jewish businessmen or what I call silly jokes. Sometimes, I signal the category, but at other times I let similar jokes follow one another naturally. And sometimes, in the middle of a category, I insert a joke that I was reminded of by the previous joke, even though it has no genre connection.

Which brings me to something important. When you get together and tell jokes, one joke reminds you of another, and that's how the conversation proceeds. You hear a joke and it reminds you of another one. If—or, rather, when—that happens as you read this book (and laugh), I hope you will rush to write down your joke—otherwise, you will forget it—and send it to me at MOMENT magazine, 4710 41st St., N.W., Washington, DC 20016; or e-mail at moment@momentmag.com; or fax at (202) 364-2636. In future editions of this book, if we use your joke, you will not only receive credit, but a free, 2-year subscription to MOMENT magazine, the leading and largest independent Jewish magazine in the country.

In the introduction to their widely and justifiably popular *The Big Book of Jewish Humor*, William Novak and Moshe Waldoks tell us that they "contacted dozens of friends, acquaintances, Jewish professionals, rabbis, joke collectors, and other interested parties. Our hope was to collect good jokes that had never before appeared in print." They even put notices in Jewish newspapers and the *New York Times Book*

Review. "The results," they tell us, "were disappointing. In all, we received close to a hundred letters, but we found very few jokes that were both new and good."

That's not been our experience. New jokes are always developing out of new situations in which Jews find themselves. (One of the sections in this book is a kind of history of Jewish jokes; I'll bet you haven't heard the latest one.) New situations in which Jews find themselves give rise to new jokes.

Novak and Waldoks also say that "all humor collections borrow from their predecessors." That is surely the case here. There is not a single joke here that I made up. Sometimes I know whose joke I copied. But often I don't. Where I know, I have given credit in the acknowledgments. But in not a single case has the person acknowledged actually claimed to have made up the joke. So the question is, who first told the joke? No one seems to know.

Novak and Waldoks say that they rewrote all the jokes they included in their book. That is true to some extent here, but when I found a particularly good telling by say, Joseph Telushkin or Leo Rosten or by Novak and Waldoks themselves, I simply copied it in its pristine form, with a doff of the hat to express my thanks.

So dive in—and enjoy. And let me hear from you. Telling jokes is a two-way street.

Hershel Shanks
Editor, MOMENT Magazine

1

This joke goes back to the late '40s. Two Jewish partners are talking:

Sam: What do you think of the Taft-Hartley bill?

Jake: Aw, the hell with it. Pay it.

Why is this joke Jewish? I don't know. Because it is (not simply because the partners are Jewish). It sounds Jewish. Here's another version of the same joke, which isn't Jewish:

President Clinton was asked to comment on the abortion bill. "I'll pay it," he said.

Since that joke isn't Jewish, I won't count it. The next joke is numbered 2, not 3. Actually, it's the same joke, but it's Jewish.

2

Sadie: What d'ya think of Red China?

Gussie: It won't go with your pink tablecloth, Sadie.

All right. So I'll give you the same joke again—and won't count it:

Sadie: What d'ya think of the Common Market?

Gussie: I still like the A & P.

Which reminds me of a story about the late great mathematician
Jon von Neumann whose work led the way to computers:

Professor von Neumann was explaining a complicated
mathematical theorem to a student and giving the proof of
it, consisting of an enormously complex equation that he
wrote on the blackboard. The student was honest: "I'm sorry,
Professor von Neumann, I don't understand it."

The professor thought for a while, scratched his head and
then again wrote the same formula on the blackboard.

"I still don't understand it, Professor von Neumann."

Again the professor cogitated and then wrote the formula on
the blackboard—for the third time.

The student still didn't understand.

The professor was exasperated: "I've done it for you three
different ways, and you still don't understand it."

I've told you the same joke four different ways, and you probably still don't think it's funny.

Speaking of Professor von Neumann, who was notoriously absent-minded, a student stopped him in the hall with a question. The professor answered the question, the student was satisfied, expressed his gratitude, and started to walk away, when the professor stopped him.

"Which way was I going?" he asked.

"That way," the student pointed.

"Ah, then I've had my lunch."

I won't count that one either. On to number 3.

3

It's hard to tell sometimes if a joke is Jewish. Sometimes it isn't even Jewish, but it becomes Jewish because it's told by a Jewish comedian. Here's a joke that's not Jewish, but you can't imagine a non-Jewish comedian telling it. It has to be told very quickly—five seconds. If you take ten seconds to tell it, it's not a Jewish joke:

Man goes to a doctor.

Doctor says, "You're sick."

Man says, "I want a second opinion."

"OK. You're ugly, too."

4

All right, here is a specifically Jewish joke. It takes us back to the days of President Bush.

The President was furious that every discussion, no matter how private, about Israel or anything that involved Jews, immediately became public. Determined to find the source of the leak, he instructed both the FBI and the CIA to investigate. Their joint report came back that the Jews had a network called "*shul*" that was impossible to infiltrate. That was where information was exchanged. To crack the leak, infiltrate the *shul.*

Bush decided that he would handle the matter himself. He called in the head of the FBI's disguise department, who dressed him in a *kittel,* put a *shtreimel* on his head, gave him a long beard and even fake *peyos.*

From an unmarked car, he departed a block from an appropriate Washington *shul.* He walked in undetected and sat himself among the crowd. After a few minutes, in accordance with his instructions, he turned to his neighbor and, in a perfect Yiddish inflection, said, "So? Nu-u-u?

"Sha!" came the vehement response. "*Der president kommt!*" (The president is coming!)

Although this joke is clearly Jewish, involving, as it does, a shul and Yiddish, still it doesn't involve any specific Jewish traits—except to the extent that Jews can find out what is going on. But it is funny. I find it hilarious, especially when told right (the punch line in a scolding manner—that makes it clearly Jewish).

Incidentally, a *kittel* is a kaftan worn by ultra-Orthodox Jews; a *shtreimel* is a broad-brimmed fur-trimmed hat, and *peyos* are earlocks. If you don't know what a *shul* is, you better stop reading this book.

I told this joke to a woman I know very well (you guessed it) and she didn't understand it. I found it difficult to explain why it was funny. In a way, it is what I call a silly joke. It makes no sense. That's why it is funny.

The funniest joke I ever heard is a silly one.

In a movie, Groucho Marx is pretending he's a doctor.

He takes the pulse of a sick man, holding the man's wrist and looking at his watch. Finally, Groucho says, "Either my watch has stopped or this man is dead."

It's hilarious, but it makes absolutely no sense. The reason it's so funny is that the more you think about it, the more nonsensical you realize it is.

5

Actually, life in *shul* can, as everyone knows, be quite contentious, as the following jokes illustrate.

Sam Meyers had an operation, and Irving Gold, the synagogue secretary, visited him in the hospital:

"I bring you the good wishes of our Board of Trustees," he said, "that you should get well and live to be a hundred and twenty! And that's an official resolution—passed by a vote of 14 to 7."

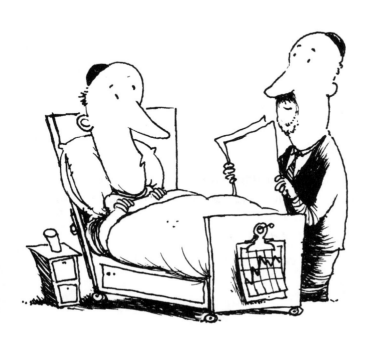

6

It was an old *shul* and the rabbi was new. When the congregation came to the *Shma*, half the congregation would rise and the other half would remain seated. The half that stood began yelling at the other half to stand: "It is the tradition in this shul to stand for the *Shma*." And the half that remained seated yelled at the other half to sit down: "It is the tradition in this shul to remain seated for the *Shma*."

Although the new rabbi was learned in the law and the commentaries, he didn't know what to do. Finally, the congregation suggested they consult the housebound 98-year-old rabbi who was still fully in control mentally; he would remember the tradition and thus be able to settle the argument.

At the appointed time, members of each faction and the new rabbi went to see the elderly sage who would surely remember what the original tradition was.

The leader of those who stood spoke first: "Isn't it the tradition in this *shul* to stand for the *Shma*?"

"No, that is not the tradition," said the old man.

Delighted with this answer, the leader of those who remained seated said: "It's the tradition in this *shul* to remain seated during the *Shma*, isn't it?"

"No, that is not the tradition."

Then the new rabbi pleaded with the old man: "But we cannot go on like this. Whenever we get to the *Shma*, half the congregation yells at the other half to sit down and the other half yells at those seated to stand up."

"Aha," said the wise old rabbi, "*that* is the tradition."

7

Two members of a congregation have been feuding for years. On Yom Kippur eve, just before the *Kol Nidre* service, the rabbi brings the two men together in his office.

"You must make peace," he commands. "What is the point of going into synagogue and asking God to forgive you when you can't even forgive your fellow man?"

The men are both moved. They hug and promise that they will not fight anymore.

When services end, one of the men greets the other. "I prayed for you everything that you prayed for me."

"Starting up already?" the second man answers.

8

Probably the largest category of Jewish jokes involves Jewish traits, or supposed Jewish traits. If an anti-Semite accused us of having some of these traits, we would call him an anti-Semite, but among ourselves it's OK.

Which suggests that at least sometimes we are over-sensitive about anti-Semitism.

Which reminds me of the story of the Jewish stutterer (sounds like I'm stuttering) who applied for a job as a radio announcer.

His friend asked if he got the job:

"N-n-n-o," he replied. "Th-th-the s-s-s-sonovabitches are a-a-a-anti-Semitic!"

9

A young Jewish bookkeeper was out of a job. Looking through the want ads one day, he spotted what appeared to be a very attractive position with an import-export firm. The ad spoke of short hours, good pay, and substantial vacation benefits. But the head of the firm wanted no Jews, and the ad left no doubts about this.

Nevertheless, the young man consulted with his wife and decided to apply anyway. Bright and early the following day, he put on his good suit and went to the office of the firm. He was a pleasant-looking fellow, but his features were unmistakably Semitic, and the manager of the accounting department immediately asked him, "Aren't you Jewish?"

"No, sir," the applicant replied. "I'm Turkish. We Turks look a lot like Jews."

"Then it's all right," said the boss with relief. Then, on a whim, he said to his assistant, "Say, Bob, why don't you go down to the shipping department and get John the Turk up here. I'd like to hear a conversation in Turkish."

Now the Jew masquerading as a Turk began to squirm, and his palms began to sweat. Within a couple of minutes John the Turk was standing before him. The Jew noticed that the man standing before him seemed equally at a loss and decided to toss caution to the winds. Grasping "the Turk" warmly by the hand, he exclaimed, "*Shalom aleichem!*" To his amazement and delight, the Turk responded, "*Aleichem shalom!*"

Assured of the "Turk's" real identity, the job applicant now ventured, "*Ayo mir hoben ihm in dr'erd!* [Don't you think he ought to go to hell?]"

The "Turk" replied, "*Gevis.* [Certainly.]"

The accounting manager drew himself up and vehemently declared, "*Ich hob eich beiden in dr'erd!* [I hope you both go to hell!]"

10

During the winter of 1926, Thelma Goldstein from Chicago treated herself to her first real vacation in Florida. Being unfamiliar with the area, she wandered into a restricted hotel in northern Miami.

"Excuse me," she said to the manager. "My name is Mrs. Goldstein, and I'd like a small room for two weeks."

"I'm awfully sorry," he replied, "but all of our rooms are occupied."

Just as he said that, a man came down and checked out.

"What luck," said Mrs. Goldstein. "Now there's a room."

"Not so fast, Madam. I'm sorry, but this hotel is restricted. No Jews allowed."

"Jewish? Who's Jewish? I happen to be Catholic."

"I find that hard to believe. Let me ask you, who was the son of God?"

"Jesus, son of Mary."

"Where was he born?"

"In a stable."

"And why was he born in a stable?"

"Because some *shmuck* like you wouldn't let a Jew rent a room in his hotel!"

Actually, most of the jokes are not about traits that an anti-Semite would accuse us of, but about traits that we are proud of (and sometimes overdo or that go awry in some way), although sometimes they are about things that an anti-Semite *would* say. For example (I won't count this one):

Two retired businessmen in Florida are getting acquainted. The first explains:

"I had a small business, which suffered a terrible tragedy. A horrible fire. But fortunately I was very well insured and with the insurance money I was able to retire nicely down here."

Said the second: "I too had a small business, but there was a terrible flood that completely wiped me out. But fortunately, I too was well insured and that was how I am able to live so well in Florida."

"Really!" said the first admiringly, "How do you make a flood?"

Probably the trait most associated with Jews is their emphasis on education, especially for their children.

Two Jews meet on the Grand Concourse in the Bronx for the first time in over 25 years—since they were boys together in Russia. One of them has two young sons with him. After the usual greetings and embraces, one of them inquires about the other's sons:

"Two beautiful boys. How old are they?"

The other replies: "The doctor's five and the lawyer's three."

12

Fannie had two sons and one became a doctor. Alas, the other became a politician. For the holidays she would always go to her pride and joy, Melvin the doctor. Never to Howard the politician—despite the fact that he did well. From the city council to mayor and from there to the governor's mansion, but still she went to Melvin the doctor. Howard was elected to congress, first to the House and then to the Senate. Still mama went to Melvin. Finally, the ultimate happened: Howard was elected the first Jewish president. To the White House he went to live, the first Jewish president. "Mama, come to my house for *Pesach*," he pleaded. At last, mama agreed.

As always, she went to the hairdresser's before *Pesach*. There she could, as usual, brag with the women. "You know my son the doctor?" she said. "I'm going to his brother's for *Pesach*."

13

Although Jews emphasize education and take pride in their children, they also complain about them:

"Insanity is hereditary," claimed the late Jewish comedian Sam Levenson. "You can get it from your children."

14

Rabbi Levy was a great rabbinic scholar who continued to teach even after he became nearly blind in his later years. Nonetheless, because he knew so much of the Talmud and its commentaries by heart, he was able to continue giving his daily Talmud *shiur* (class). Unfortunately, Rabbi Levy knew the name of only one student, Bernstein, and every day he called on him to read and explain the Talmudic portion being studied. This was driving Bernstein crazy, so one morning, when Rabbi Levy said, "Nu, Bernstein, read the Talmud," the student spoke up in a falsetto voice, "Bernstein is not here today." Rabbi Levy paused a moment, then responded, "Bernstein's not here? Then you read the Talmud."

15

And then, of course, there's the overbearing Jewish mother:

A Jewish man goes to see a psychiatrist and says, "Everyone I see reminds me of my mother. My wife, the newscaster, even your secretary reminds me of my mother. I'm obsessed. I go to sleep and I dream about my mother. I wake up, can't get back to sleep and I have to go downstairs and have a glass of tea and a piece of toast.

The psychiatrist says, "What? Just one piece of toast for a big boy like you?"

This is a complicated joke. The apparently Jewish psychiatrist is talking like a Jewish mother. He's got the same problem.

16

A mother gave her son David (the lawyer) two ties for Chanukah. The next week he arrived for Shabbat dinner wearing one of the ties. His mother greeted him:

"Whatsa matter? You didn't like the other tie?"

17

Styles in Jewish jokes change, as the Jewish condition changes. Today there are not so many jokes about anti-Semitism because few Jews in America are affected by it. There are also fewer jokes about poor Jews because most Jews in this country are no longer poor. And when they are, it's not because of their Jewishness. In fact, there are probably more jokes today about Jews being rich than poor.

Consider this one about two retired Jews talking in Miami Beach:

"I just got myself a new car."

"Really? What kind did you get?"

"Blue."

End of joke. You didn't get it? Of course, it was a Caddy. The only question was one of color.

18

Compare this to the days when Jews lived in impoverished shtetls in Eastern Europe:

When a Jew eats a chicken and it isn't Shabbos, either the Jew or the chicken is sick.

19

Two beggars were sitting next to each other on a street corner in Krakow. One holds a sign saying, "Please help a war veteran;" the other holds a sign saying, "Please help a poor Jew."

Even those who don't usually stop to give money to street beggars put money in the veteran's cup, happy to spite the Jew sitting next to him. In a short time, the veteran's cup is full, he pockets the money, and once again holds out his cup.

One kind man, watching all this, decides to give some money to both beggars, and to give the Jew some advice:

"You should change your sign! You know, in this town you won't get much money as a Jew."

As the good man walks away, the Jew turns to the veteran and says, "Yossele, even the good ones want to tell us how to run our business!"

Also in the old days, there was a distinct Jewish pecking order, depending on where you came from. The pecking order also varied, depending on who was telling it. No matter how I tell it, therefore, I will be insulting someone, so just consider this arbitrary:

The Galitzianers [from Galicia] talk to the Litvaks [from Lithuania], the Litvaks talk to the Rusheshers [Russians], the Rusheshers talk to the Germans, and the Germans talk to God.

Did you ever see a Galitzianer cookbook? It starts out, "Steal three eggs . . . ."

21

After months of negotiations, a Jewish scholar from Kiev is granted permission to visit Moscow. He boards the train and finds an empty seat. At the next stop a young man gets on and sits next to him. The scholar looks at the young man and thinks:

This fellow doesn't look like a peasant, and if he isn't a peasant, he probably comes from this district. If he comes from this district, he must be Jewish because this is, after all, a Jewish district. On the other hand, if he's a Jew, where could he be going? I'm the only one in our district who has permission to travel to Moscow.

Wait—just outside Moscow there is a little village called Samvet, and you don't need special permission to go there.

But why would he be going to Samvet? He's probably going to visit somebody there, but how many Jewish families are there in Samvet? Only two—the Mermelsteins and the Steinbergs. The Mermelsteins are a terrible family, so he must be visiting the Steinbergs. But why is he going?

The Steinbergs have only girls, so maybe he's their son-in-law. But if he is, then which daughter did he marry? Sarah married that nice lawyer from Budapest and Esther married a businessman from Zhatomir, so it must be Sarah's husband. Which means that his name is Alexander Cohen, if I'm not mistaken. But if he comes from Budapest, with all the anti-Semitism they have there, he must have changed his name. What's the Hungarian equivalent of Cohen? Kovacs. But if he changed his name, he must have some special status. What could it be? A doctorate from the university.

At this point the scholar turns to the young man and says, "How do you do, Dr. Kovacs?"

"Very well, thank you, sir," answers the startled passenger. "But how is it that you know my name?"

"Oh," replies the scholar, "It was obvious."

22

Nazi Germany, horrible as it was, produced its share of jokes.
Humor has always been one Jewish way of coping:

At a mass meeting in Berlin, Hitler was haranguing the crowd, shrieking:

"And who is responsible for all of our troubles?," expecting the crowd to shout "The Jews."

However, a little Jew shouts back, "The bicycle riders!"

Hitler looks up, astonished. "Why the bicycle riders?" he asks.

"Why the Jews?" replies the Jew.

23

Here's another one from the Nazi period:

An elderly Jew is sitting in a park in Berlin reading a Nazi newspaper. A friend walks by and notices.

"How can you be doing this?"

"Well," explains the older man, "It says here that all Jews are rich, we're all very powerful, we stick together, and help each other become more rich and powerful. Where else can you get that kind of good news?"

24

Communist Russia has also produced its share of Jewish jokes. Here's one of the best:

One cold winter morning in Moscow a rumor went around that a certain butcher shop would have meat for sale. Within minutes a long line had formed outside of the shop. At 9:00 a.m., the butcher comes out and announces, "Well, comrades, there's not enough meat for everybody. All Jews must leave the line." They do, and the line gets a little shorter.

At noon, the butcher comes out again and says, "Comrades, there's not enough meat. Anybody who is not a member of the Party must leave immediately." Many people leave and the line is shortened.

At 3:00 p.m., it's still freezing and the butcher comes out and announces, "There's still not enough meat for all of you! Everybody who did not defend Mother Russia from the fascists must leave." Again, the line grows shorter.

At 5:00 p.m., the butcher announces, "There's still not enough! All those who did not help liberate our country from the Czar must leave!" This leaves only two old shivering men.

Finally, at 9:00 p.m., the butcher comes out and says, "There isn't any meat."

The old men move slowly away, grumbling, and one says to the other, "Those Jews always get the best of everything!"

Once the Jews were allowed to leave the Soviet Union and come to Israel, a new set of jokes arose. Here's my favorite—from the cafes of Tel Aviv:

Question: How do you tell a Russian pianist?

Answer: He doesn't have a violin case under his arm.

In an earlier time, when the United States and the Soviet Union were attempting to thaw out the cold war by cultural exchanges, violinist Isaac Stern remarked:

"They send us their Jews from Odessa and we send them our Jews from Odessa."

26

Some Jewish jokes are very culture bound. They're funny for a time. But they won't last—because they won't be understood. If explained, they won't be funny. This one's fading because it relies on the fading custom of Jewish families to "eat out" at Chinese restaurants on Sunday night to give Mom a break from the kitchen. With the recent craze for healthful eating, as well as a variety of new restaurants, the Sunday night Chinese family meal is no longer the standard ritual.

"The Jewish people have observed their 5758th year as a people," the Hebrew teacher informed his class.

"Consider that the Chinese have observed only their 4695th. What does this mean to you?"

After a reflective pause, one student volunteered, "Well, for one thing, the Jews had to do without Chinese food for 1063 years."

27

Speaking of Chinese restaurants, how about this one involving Chinese waiters:

Sam was eating in a Lower East Side restaurant. The food was delicious. The service surprisingly excellent. The waiters, however, were all Chinese—but speaking perfect Yiddish.

When he went up to the cash register to pay the check, Sam asked the owner, "Where did you find these Chinese waiters who speak perfect Yiddish?"

"Sh, Sh," he replied with his index finger to his lips. "They think it's English."

Jewish waiters, on the other hand, especially in Jewish restaurants, are known for their brashness, not to say impudence:

Two men came into a restaurant on the Lower East Side of Manhattan. The first one asks for tea.

The second also asks for tea. "And make sure the glass is clean," he tells the waiter.

The waiter returns with two glasses of tea. "Two teas: Who gets the clean glass?"

29

Shloimy had never been to an automat before. He stood feeding the apple pie slot with coins when his friend Moshe tried to stop him. "Shloimy, what are you doing? For God's sake, stop. You already have eight pieces of pie."

"I should stop at a time like this," he replies, "when I'm on such a winning streak?"

If the joke about Sunday night at the Chinese restaurant is fading, here is one that hasn't quite arrived. It's based on the recent return to tradition:

The Ostroffs named their new baby Shlomo—after his grandfather Sean.

31

It's time for a real howler. Like many Jewish jokes, this one is based on Yiddish—or rather on a Yiddish accent.

They were casting for a new Broadway production of Hamlet. The producer, the director, and the backers were all there to watch the auditions. The theater was dark except for the spotlight on the stage that revealed the next actor in line:

"I'm de expot act-her. I'm vanting to do Hamlet," he said with a thick Yiddish accent.

"Wait a minute," said the director, "You want to play Hamlet?"

"Natchly,' he said. "I know actin'."

He was quickly shunted aside, but at the end of the day there was still time for one more audition, so they decided to let him give a demonstration of his "actin'."

In a full, mellow voice that filled the theater he began to intone the Act I soliloquy in the purest Oxford accent: "O that this too, too solid flesh would melt, thaw and resolve itself into a dew . . . "

Astounded, the director interrupted: "Wait a minute! What is this? How did you do that?"

Back in his Yiddish accent, the actor replied, "I told you I vas an expot. Dat's actin'."

We're accustomed to actors simulating a Yiddish accent, but why shouldn't someone with a Yiddish accent, who is an expert actor, be able to simulate a Shakespearean accent? The humor derives from looking at things from the other direction.

The same is true in the following remark:

"Christmas comes late this year."

We're accustomed to hearing that Rosh Hashanah comes late—or early—this year. Sometimes it comes in September, sometime in October. But actually it comes at the same time every year—on the first of Tishri. It's Christmas that is always moving around—sometimes in Kislev, sometimes in Tevet. You never know, and it's hard to keep track of—if your standard is the Jewish calendar.

It all depends on what your standard is.

Louis Finkelstein, chancellor of the Jewish Theological Seminary of America, was on his way to Rome as one of President John Kennedy's representatives to the coronation of Pope Paul VI. Finkelstein, of course, maintained a strictly kosher diet. On a stopover in Paris, he was taken to a kosher restaurant by a group of local rabbis. Quipped Dr. Finkelstein upon leaving, "I can't understand all this fuss people make about French cooking. We have the same things at home."

32

Naturally in preparation for this book, I read the three most popular collections of Jewish jokes—Joseph Telushkin's *Jewish Humor*, Leo Rosten's *The Joys of Yiddish* and William Novak and Moshe Waldoks's *The Big Book of Jewish Humor*. All of them had this one; in this telling, I've tried to combined the best elements of each:

An elderly Jewish couple, on their way to a vacation in Hawaii, get into an argument about the correct pronunciation of Hawaii: he is sure it is Havaii, but she maintains it is Hawaii.

When they get off the plane, they hurry over to the first native they see and say, "Aloha! How do you pronounce the name of this island: Hawaii or Havaii?"

"Havaii," the man replies.

"Thank you," the husband says triumphantly.

"You're velcome," the man replies.

33

Maybe because my father owned a shoe store, I've always liked jokes about Jewish businessmen—their often warm relationship with one another, their shared *tsuris*, their complaints—and their cleverness. The following jokes reflect all of this and perhaps explain why they are Jewish jokes.

Two Jewish businessmen got to discussing Albert Einstein and his baffling theory of relativity. One of them suggested this analogy by way of explanation: "If you sit on a hot stove for a second, it will seem like an hour. But if a beautiful woman sits on your lap for an hour, it will seem like a second."

Replies the other, "And from this he makes a living?"

34

After a terrible automobile accident, Chaim Cohen, in obvious pain, is riding in the ambulance on his way to the hospital.

The concerned paramedic asks him, "Are you comfortable?"

Mr. Cohen shrugs and says, "I make a living."

> Is this the same joke as the last one? Think about it. Then you'll know what makes it Jewish.

35

A woman walks into Rosenfeld's bakery and asks, "How much are bagels?"

"Three twenty-five a dozen," comes the reply.

"That's pretty high," says the woman. "Eagerman sells them for two-seventy."

"So buy from Eagerman."

"I can't," says the woman. "He's out of bagels."

"Aha!" says Rosenfeld. "When I'm out of bagels, I also sell for two-seventy."

36

Two Jewish businessmen meet on the street and begin to chat. Says the first: "How's business?"

Krechtzs the second, "Eh."

"Well, for this time of year, that's not so bad!"

37

"You see this vest?" said the tailor. "I sell it for $25. Costs me $27 to make."

"So how do you stay in business?"

"I make it up on volume."

38

Cohen is walking down the street and sees his friend Feinberg coming in the opposite direction, wearing the most beautiful sport coat he has ever seen.

"Feinberg, that's a great sport coat you're wearing. Where did you get it?"

"From Rabinowitz, the tailor," Feinberg replies.

"I gotta have one. How much did it cost?"

"Ten thousand dollars."

Cohen doesn't believe it for a moment. He knows Feinberg is trying to discourage him.

Cohen immediately goes to Rabinowitz the tailor. "You know my friend Feinberg. He bought from you a sport coat. I would like one just like it. But how much does it cost?"

Without blinking an eye, the tailor responds: "Ten thousand dollars."

"Ten thousand dollars? Are you crazy? Ten thousand dollars for a sport coat?"

"Look, sit down, let me tell you about this sport coat. This is not a sport coat; this is a work of art. This is a sport coat for you and for you alone. When you order this sport coat, I immediately fax Kyoto to take silkworms out of the darkness to spin the finest silk for your garment. The silk itself is dyed in India. At the same time, we telex Adelaide, Australia to climb the highest mountain peak where the shepherds choose a young sheep with the finest wool; the wool is then woven in Scotland."

Cohen is impressed, but Rabinowitz is just getting started. "Did you see the buttons on that sport coat? When you order that sport coat, I myself fly to Luzon in the Philippines, hire a diver and we go to the deepest part of the Mariana Trench to find the most lustrous oysters for the buttons on your sport jacket."

Cohen is, by this time, blown away, but Rabinowitz continues: "Now let me tell you what we do with all this. The materials are all sent to our factory in Paris, where Yves Saint Laurent personally designs a jacket for you based on photographs of you taken by Richard Avedon. These pictures are taken from every angle so that they capture your very essence. From this you get a sport jacket that conforms to your very essence and fits like a heavenly garment."

Cohen doesn't need any time to think; he's convinced; he wants one. "You know, when you think about it, with all that goes into it, ten thousand dollars is not such a bad price," Cohen says. "There's only one problem: I need it for a bar mitzvah on Shabbos."

Without missing a beat, Rabinowitz replies, "You'll have it. YOU'LL HAVE IT!"

This is a joke about negotiating, but it's really about much more. How much more is for you to decide and decipher.

Jake: Sam, have I got a deal for you. I've got a $25,000 elephant and it's yours for ten grand."

Sam: But Jake, I don't need an elephant. I live in an apartment.

Jake: All right. Make it $7,500 and it's yours.

Sam: No, you don't understand Jake. It's not the price. It's just that I wouldn't know what to do with an elephant. How can I buy an elephant for a one-bedroom apartment?

Jake: Sam, you're a tough bargainer. Give me five grand and walk away with it.

Sam: Make it two for $7,000 and you've got a deal.

40

Two old Jews, retired businessmen, are sitting on a bench in Central Park. After an hour, one of them moans, groans, shifts his body this way and that, and after no small effort struggles to his feet. Says the other, "Vadda u runnin?"

41

In its way, the previous joke is related to this one. But it also harks back to the days when Jews managed to get along by making themselves nearly invisible:

Sam and Irving are facing the firing squad. The executioner comes forward to place the blindfold on them. Sam disdainfully and proudly refuses, tearing the thing from his face. Irving turns to him and pleads: "Please, Sam, don't make trouble!"

42

If the previous joke is self-effacing, many jokes show how clever Jews are, especially in comparison to non-Jews. Here's a favorite of mine. Even though it's very old, it's still very funny.

In the early 1900s, an old Jew is traveling alone in his compartment on the Trans-Siberian Railroad. The train stops and an officer in the czar's army gets on. He and the Jew travel for a while in silence. Suddenly the officer grabs the Jew by the lapels and demands: "Tell me, why are you Jews so much brighter than everyone else?"

The Jew is silent a moment, then responds: "It's because of the herring we eat."

The officer quiets down and the trip resumes. Soon the Jew takes out a piece of herring and starts to eat it. The officer asks him: "How many more pieces of herring do you have?"

"A dozen."

"How much do you want for them?"

"Twenty rubles." A big sum of money.

The officer takes out the money and gives it to the Jew. The old man gives him the herring, and the officer takes a bite. Suddenly he stops. "This is ridiculous," he says. "In Moscow I could have bought all this herring for a few kopecks."

"You see," says the Jew, "It's already working."

43

The previous joke went back a hundred years. This one goes back about half that:

Sam and Jake had been millionaires. Now it was the depth of the depression. They had not seen each other since October 29, 1929, when they had davened together on Yom Kippur. That was Black Monday, the day the stock market crashed, beginning the worst depression in American history. Now, three years later, they were paupers, but they recognized each other immediately. Each was selling apples from a cart. They fell into each other's arms. Then they got to reminiscing and finally reached the events of October 29.

Said Sam: You see, Jake, we leave it to the *goyim* for one day and this is what happens.

44

Abie sold *tallesim* and *tephillin*—and business was bad. He couldn't make a living. Finally, he decided that he would have to expand his product line and sell Christian religious supplies. He looked in the Yellow Pages and located a wholesaler of Christian religious supplies, dialed the number, and said:

"Hello, this is Abie Cohen and I would like to buy twelve dozen crosses."

The voice on the other end: "Mit or mitout Jesuses?"

45

A rabbi and a priest are riding on a train, talking, when the porter comes by selling ham sandwiches. The priest buys, but the rabbi passes, explaining that he does not eat ham.

"You've never had a ham sandwich?"

"No," the rabbi replies.

"You really ought to try it."

The discussion goes on. The rabbi then shows him a picture of his wife and asks if the priest is married.

"No, it's against my religion for a priest to marry."

"Have you never had a woman?"

"No, never," the priest replies.

"Really? You ought to try it. It's better than ham."

The priest was going away for two weeks and had no one to take confessions, so he went across the street and asked the rabbi from the synagogue if he would help out. The rabbi was glad to oblige, but he wasn't sure he knew how. The priest suggested that he come over and simply sit with him for a few confessions and he would get the hang of it.

On the other side of the screen a man came in while the priest and the rabbi listened.

"I have sinned, father—with a woman."

Priest: You are forgiven, my son. Put $20 in the collection box and sin no more.

A second man came in. His sin was worse: "I have sinned, father, with women—not only with one woman but with two."

Priest: You are forgiven, my son. Put $20 in the collection box and sin no more.

Still a third man came in—this time confessing to sinning with three women. Again the priest forgave him, instructed the man to put $20 in the collection box and to sin no more.

By this time, the rabbi thought he understood and the priest left on his vacation.

Promptly the next morning, the rabbi was in the confession booth, ready to take his first confession.

"I have sinned, O father—with a woman."

Rabbi: Put $20 in the collection box and have two more women. We're running a special this week—three for $20.

47

How do we know Jesus was Jewish?

1. He was thirty, unmarried, and still living with his family.

2. He went into his father's business.

3. He thought his mother was a virgin.

4. And his mother thought he was God.

If this seems a bit disrespectful, Jews can also make jokes about their own God.

48

This is a very funny joke, but two caveats apply: It really depends on how it is told; the punchline must be delivered casually, very un-God-addressing-like. In this joke God uses his godly powers like a naughty little boy; that's not the way he's supposed to act; but that's what makes it funny—God's just like anybody else. The second caveat: It contains a dirty word that I softened in this telling.

God and Moses are playing golf. God tees off—a terrible slice, skimming high off into the woods, when suddenly a cloud appears in the sky. A bird flies out of the sky, catches the ball in its beak, and drops it back on the course. As it begins to come to a rest, a rabbit dashes out of the woods, scurries over the ball, pushing it on to the green, rolling toward the hole. As it rolls to a stop beside the hole, a gopher pokes his head out of the ground, hits the ball with his nose—and the ball drops into the hole. A hole in one.

Moses looks at God skeptically and says, "Aw right, ya' wanna screw around or ya' wanna play golf?"

49

Rabbi Finkelstein was an avid golfer and played at every opportunity. He was so addicted to the game that if he didn't play he would get withdrawal symptoms.

One Yom Kippur, he thought to himself, "Who will be hurt if I go out and play a few rounds during the recess. Nobody will be the wiser and I'll be back in time for services." At the conclusion of the *Musaf* service, Rabbi Finkelstein snuck out of the synagogue and headed straight for the golf course. Looking down upon him were Moshe Rabeinu and God.

Moshe said, "Look what that Jew is doing—and a Rabbi yet."

God replied, "I'll teach him a lesson."

Rabbi Finkelstein teed off. The ball careened off a tree, struck a rock, flew across a stream and landed in the hole. A HOLE IN ONE!

Moshe yelled, "Is this how you're going to teach him a lesson? A hole in one, he got."

With a glint in his eye, God replied, "Who's he gonna tell?"

50

Some Jews try to out-do each other in holiness. It's a form of upstaging:

Haim ha-Tzadik passed to the next world, where they were so happy to have him that they made a grand banquet in his honor. The waiters were angels and the main dish was the great fish Leviathan.

Haim called over one of the waiters and inquired, "Who's the *mashgiach** here?"

"Here the Lord himself is the *mashgiach*," replied the angel full of rectitude.

"I'll take the fruit plate," Haim replied.

*The man who makes sure everything is kosher.

51

A Jewish boy is going off to college and his father says to him: "Look, we've never been a religious family, so I'm not expecting you to become suddenly religious. But promise me one thing: You won't marry a *shiksa*."

The boy promises.

Sure enough, his senior year he falls in love with a non-Jewish girl. She loves him too, but he tells her he can't marry her because she's not Jewish.

"Don't worry," she says. "I'll convert."

After serious study, the girl converts. They marry and go off on their honeymoon. Four weeks later, back at home Saturday morning at 8:00 a.m., the phone rings at their house. It's the boy's father. He's livid. "You know the last Saturday of every month we go over the books at the office. Why aren't you down here?"

"I can't come," the boy says. "My wife says it's forbidden. It's Shabbat. We're heading off to *shul*."

"I told you not to marry a *shiksa*," the father screams.

52

A tour in the Negev. The bus stops at the *Makhtesh Ramon*, a huge, vastly impressive crater. As the people get out of the bus, one man—there is one in every tour group—runs around everyone else to be next to where he thinks the tour guide will stand, overlooking the crater. But, unfortunately, he gets too close and falls off the edge. No one even notices that he has fallen off. Down, down, he falls, until he manages to grasp a root sticking out of the side of the crater. In terror, he looks up and cries: "Is anybody up there?"

Only silence.

Again he calls: "Is anybody up there?"

Again silence.

A third time he calls. He looks up in desperation, barely able to hold on, when he sees a cloud in the sky, and a voice comes out of the cloud: "Do you believe?"

"Oh, yes, dear God. I believe."

"Are you sure you believe?"

"Oh, yes, dear God, I believe in perfect faith," he screams.

Then the voice speaks again, softly: "Let go!"

Silence.

Then: "Is anybody else up there?"

53

A Jewish girl brings her fiancé home to meet her parents. Her father takes the young man aside.

"So tell me," asks the father, "What do you do for a living?"

"I am a Torah scholar," the young man replies.

"A Torah scholar," the father says, "Wonderful, but what are your plans?"

"I will be a Torah scholar," answers the young man.

"And tell me," asks the father, "How will you provide for my daughter?"

"I will study the Torah," the young man replied, "and God will provide for us."

"Yes, and how will you provide for, God willing, my grandchildren?"

"I will study the Torah," the young man replied, "and God will provide for us."

Later, the girl's mother asks, "So, *nu*, how did it go?"

"Well," said the father, "The bad news is he has no visible means of support, but the good news is he thinks I'm God."

54

A man brings some very fine material to a tailor and asks him to make a pair of pants. When he comes back a week later, the pants are not ready. Two weeks later, they are still not ready. Finally, after six weeks, the pants are ready. The man tries them on. They fit perfectly. Nonetheless, when it comes time to pay, he can't resist a jibe at the tailor.

"You know," he says, "it took God only six days to make the world. And it took you six weeks to make just one pair of pants."

"Ah," the tailor says. "But look at this pair of pants, and look at the world!"

Here, in effect, is the same joke with a different setting, but it isn't Jewish. Nevertheless, compare the punchlines.

Jed, a black man in Alabama, decided to do something about the field at the corner of Oak and Elm. It was overgrown with weeds, thorns and thistles, to say nothing of the garbage that had collected there over the years. Jed transformed it into a beautiful, well-tended garden full of beautiful flowers and healthful vegetables. One day while he is watering his creation, the preacher comes by and congratulates him: "Jed, it's wonderful what you and the good Lord have done with this field."

"I don't want to take nothing away from the good Lord," Jed replies, "but you shoulda seen this place when he was working it hisself."

55

A little boy comes home from religious school (formerly *cheder*). "What did you learn today?" asks his father.

"Oh, the teacher told us the story about General Moses, how General Moses was leading all the Jews out of Egypt, with General Pharoah's Egyptians hot on their trail. And there was the Red Sea in front of Moses, so he dropped an atomic bomb! Bang! So the waters parted, the Jews got across, and the Egyptians were all drowned."

"Is that what the teacher told you?" gasped the father.

The boy shrugged. "Nope, but if I told it to you the way he did, Pop, you'd never believe it."

56

An assimilated, secular Jewish family moved to a small town where the best school was the local Catholic school. Believing in education, the family enrolled their youngest child.

After the first day of school, the youngster comes home and says, "Daddy, did you know that God is really three, and there's a son and a Holy Ghost and his son died for our sins?"

The distraught father replies, "Listen, there's only one God, and we don't believe in him."

This is not so much a joke about God as about secular Jews: The God they don't believe in is the Jewish God.

57

A new version of Creation has been found among the Dead Sea Scrolls—a feminist version. Instead of woman being created from the rib of a man, man was created from a part of woman. Here is how the story goes, translated from the Hebrew; unfortunately, the text is fragmentary and this is all that has been preserved:

". . . and God created Woman, giving her three breasts to succor her young . . . But the Woman complained to God, saying, 'Lord, I am not made to birth whole litters. I need but two breasts . . . And God said, 'O Woman, thou speaketh wisely. I created thee with Wisdom' . . . Suddenly there was thunder and lightening and the heavens split apart . . . When the sun came out again, the Woman was standing there holding her third breast in her hand . . . 'Now what shall I do with this useless boob?' the Woman asked God. 'From the boob I shall make thee a companion and he shall be called Man.' And so it was . . ."

58

Iz shver tzuzein a Yid. It's tough to be a Jew, goes the old Yiddish saying. But, today, it really isn't. It's like being a member of a small, exclusive, privileged club. Yet today, as always, some Jews want to leave the fold, to shed their Jewishness, to blend into the mainstream. But it can't be done. That is the burden of a number of Jewish jokes.

Late in life, Chaim decides he's had it with Judaism and decides to convert to Christianity. His wife's efforts to dissuade him are fruitless. One day he comes home to announce that the deed is done. He has converted and is now a Christian. The next morning his wife gets out of bed; as usual, Chaim is up before her. And there he is davening in his *tephillin*!

Sarah: I didn't want you to become a Christian, but now that you've done it, what are you doing laying *tephillin*?

Chaim knocks his head with his palm and exclaims: *"Oy, goyische kop."*

This joke, too, depends on how it is told. The punchline must be delivered with genuine surprise. A *goyische kop* is, of course, a derogatory reference—a Jewish head is smart; a non-Jewish head isn't, at least not as smart.

59

Mort Abramowitz leaves his Manhattan office one weekend and en route home via Fifth Avenue he comes upon a long line. Upon inquiring, the last person in line tells him that they are giving a great gift to all those in line. Never one to forego a freebee, Mort remains in line until, to his horror, he winds up in front of St. John's Church where a priest is busy converting people. Mort cries out to the priest that he's made a terrible mistake and will just leave. The priest whispers back angrily, "Don't make me look bad. Go through the motions." Mort accedes, then runs to catch the train to Larchmont to tell his family what has just happened.

He runs into the house crying, "Maxine, Maxine, guess what happened to me." His wife, however, passes him swiftly departing through the front door, saying, "Mort, I'm late for my Maj game. I'll talk to you when I get back."

Disgruntled, he runs upstairs to tell his daughter. He bursts into her room moaning, "Karen Beth, you won't believe what happened to your father!" His little angel, however, is obviously in the midst of an important telephone conversation, and hisses, "Dad, dad, I've been waiting for this boy to call me for three months. I'll talk with you when I get off."

Thoroughly nettled, he runs downstairs and out to the garage where his son is working under the hood of his car. "Alvin, Alvin," he cries. "Guess what happened to your father?" Alvin, however, distractedly asks, "Dad, I am trying to get the timing right, would you hand me that wrench on the table?"

Mort reaches over for the wrench, slaps it into his son's hand, and mutters, "Whaddya know; I'm a *goy* for one hour and already I hate three Jews."

60

Yankel Rabinovich is jogging down Sixth Avenue, when it starts to rain. He looks around and sees a sign on a building, "Empire State Athletic Club," so he goes in to apply for membership.

"What is your name?" asks the clerk.

"Yankel Rabinovich."

"And what do you do, Mr. Rabinovich?" asks the clerk.

"I'm a tailor."

"And what is your religion?"

"I'm Jewish."

"We have no openings," says the clerk brusquely.

Yankel decides life would be much easier as a gentile. He converts to Christianity, learns to play golf, and changes his name. A year later, he walks into the Athletic Club to apply for membership once again.

"What is your name?" asks the clerk.

"William Farnsworth III," replies Yankel.

"And what do you do, Mr. Farnsworth," asks the clerk.

"I am a professional golfer," says Yankel.

"And what is your religion?" asks the clerk.

"I'm a *goy*."

61

This one goes back to the late '40s.

Shloimy—now Stafford—had finally become a British citizen. When his childhood friend from Vilna came to visit him, he expected to find Shloimy overjoyed. Instead, he found him disconsolate.

"Shloimy, I mean Stafford, I thought you would be happy. You have what you always wanted. You're a British citizen. What's the matter?"

"We lost India."

Charles Steinmetz, a hunchback who discovered the basic properties of electromagnetism, was showing his garden to a convert from Judaism who told him, "I, too, was once a Jew." Steinmetz replied, "And I was once a hunchback."

62

A nicely dressed young man with horn-rimmed glasses sits down beside an elderly Jewish lady on the subway and opens a book. From the corner of her eye, she inspects him and finally asks: "You're Jewish?"

Young man: No ma'am, I'm not.

Elderly woman (hesitates, looks from the corner of her eye): Tell the troots.

Young man: I'm sorry ma'am, but I don't happen to be Jewish.

Elderly woman (after more hesitation and more glances): Tell the troots.

In an effort to stop the questioning and get back to his reading, the young man finally decides to tell her what she wants to hear: "OK, yes, I'm Jewish."

Elderly woman: You know, you don't look a bit Jewish.

63

An assimilated Jewish woman from the Midwest is visiting Philadelphia and gets on a bus. A few stops later a man with a wide brimmed black hat, white shirt, long black coat, black pants, black shoes, and a long curly black beard gets on and sits down beside her.

The woman looks at him disgustedly. "Jews like you," she hisses at him, "give us all a bad name."

He looks up at her, puzzled, and says, "I beg your pardon, madam?"

She says, "Look at you. All in black, a beard, never take off your hat! It's Jews like you that give the rest of us a problem."

He says calmly, "I beg your pardon, madam, but I am not Jewish. I'm Amish."

The woman looks back and smiles, "How nice. You've kept your customs."

64

The Countess is lying in the magnificent Louis XIV bedroom of her imposing mansion awaiting the birth of her child. The Count, her husband, is in the drawing room playing cards with the doctor, while they await the need for the doctor's services.

"*Mon Dieu*," the mother-to-be cries from the bedroom.

"It's time," says the husband.

"Not yet," says the doctor as he shuffles the cards, "there's plenty of time."

Some time later, there is a second cry from the bedroom: "*Mein Gott.*"

The Count looks up.

Again the doctor replies, "Not yet, don't worry," as he continues to deal the cards.

Some time later still, another scream comes from the bedroom: "*Oy gevalt.*"

"Now," says the doctor, "it's time."

65

What's the difference between a Brit and a Jew? The Brit leaves without saying goodbye and the Jew says goodbye without leaving.

Another version:

Dress British, Think Yiddish.

66

Zelda Farbman, a sixty-something widow living in Boca, climbs on the bus on her way home from Publix market and discovers every seat is taken. She looks down at a young man sitting by himself. Pointing to her chest, she plaintively says to him, "Young man, if you knew what I had in here, you'd give me your seat." Embarrassed, the young man gets up and offers Zelda his place.

Next, she looks over at the woman sitting next to her, and intones mournfully, "Madam, if you knew what I had in here, you'd offer to hold my groceries." The woman sheepishly looks over and takes her packages.

Zelda next spies a woman standing and fanning herself in the un-air-conditioned bus. She makes a fist and beats her chest and whines, "Young woman, on such a hot day as today, if you had in here what I had, you'd lend me your fan." The young woman guiltily hands the instrument over to her.

Five minutes later, Zelda jumps up, grabs her groceries, hands back the fan and races to the front of the bus, asking the driver to stop at the next block. The driver responds, "Madam, that is not a stop."

Again, beating her breast, Zelda says, "If you knew what I had in here, you'd stop anywhere I asked." Grudgingly, the driver pulls over and as Zelda steps off the bus, asks her, "Madam, what exactly do you have in there?"

Looking over her shoulder, Zelda yells back, "Chutzpah!"

67

A definition of chutzpah:

A man goes to a lawyer and asks, "How much do you charge for legal advice?"

"A thousand dollars for three questions."

"Wow! Isn't that kind of expensive?"

"Yes, it is. What is your third question?"

That's chutzpah!

68

Jews are very word-y people. Probably that's why so many Jewish jokes are really plays on words. (That's the first time I've ever had the opportunity to use the plural of "a play on words.") One advantage for a book of jokes is that plays on words (that's the second time; I'm getting to like it even though it still doesn't sound right) don't depend as much on delivery. Except when a Yiddish accent is involved. That's true with the next couple of jokes. After that, we'll do some straight ones.

A woman with a heavy Yiddish accent enters a posh restaurant.

"We don't serve Jews here," the manager tells her.

"Dat's all right," she says. "I don't eat them."

Esther Shapiro was troubled. She had been happily married for many years, but still she was distraught. Being a thoroughly modern woman despite her heavy Yiddish accent, she decided to consult a psychiatrist. To help him assess her condition, he explained to her that he wanted to do some what-is-called "free association:" The doctor would say a word and she was to respond with the first thing that came into her mind. She understood.

Psychiatrist: Chair.

Mrs. Shapiro: Table.

Psychiatrist: Cup.

Mrs. Shapiro: Saucer.

Psychiatrist: Sex!

Mrs. Shapiro: Fift Evenoo. [Fifth Avenue]

70

This one doesn't depend on a Yiddish double entendre, but it is better if the punchline is told with a Yiddish accent.

Rex Smith from Dallas checked into his suite in the Waldorf-Astoria and promptly rung up the Carnegie Hall box office:

(In his Texas drawl:) "Hello, this is Rex Smith from Texas. I want two orchestra tickets for tomorrow's Van Cliburn concert."

"I'm sorry, sir, but we're all sold out for that concert."

"You don't understand, ma'am. This is Rex Smith from Texas, and I want two orchestra tickets for the Van Cliburn concert."

Same response. Another demand, only more insistent. Same response.

Threateningly, "Well, I'm going to come down there in person and we'll see if you can find two tickets to tomorrow's concert."

Rex hops in a cab and is left out on the opposite corner. He looks around, it's his first trip to New York and he's unsure where Carnegie Hall is. He finally stops an old *yidle* with a heavy accent and a violin case under his arm. "Excuse me, sir, how do I get to Carnegie Hall."

The *yidle* replies: "Practice, practice, practice."

71

A small New York park is filled with benches where elderly Jews gather in the afternoon to shmooze. It's called the Garden of Yidden.

72

A first novel entitled Mine Boy about a South African black man's life in the diamond mines enjoyed a brisk sale in Miami, where it was thought to be a Jewish mother's account of her son's accomplishments.

73

During a convention in Miami, two female delegates meet in the lobby. Sadelle falls upon Shirley's neck and they embrace, and begin to chatter away.

"Darling, you look wonderful," says Sadelle. "How come you look so good?"

"Ssh. I'll tell you a secret. I'm having an affair!"

"Really? That's marvelous! Who's catering?"

74

Question: How many Jewish grandmothers does it take to change a lightbulb?

Answer: None—"That's OK, I'll sit in the dark."

75

Abie and Rivkeh had been dating for nearly a year and he has been trying his best to convince her to sleep with him. "Ever'body does it," he urges.

"Really ever'body?"

"Really ever'body."

Finally, she relents. The next morning Abie calls to find out how she is.

"It vas voderful!" she says. "But tell me really, does ever'body do it?"

"Ever'body."

"Absolutely ever'body?"

"Absolutely ever'body."

"You know," she says, "It's too good for de *goyim*!"

76

Sadie and Rivkeh, young, but both recently widowed, finally decide to begin dating again, often comparing notes.

Sadie: You'll never guess who I have a date with Saturday night—Izzy Melnik.

Rivkeh: Izzy Melnik? I went out with him two weeks ago. He came on the dot of 7 to pick me up in a limousine. He knocked on the door with a dozen roses. He took me to the most expensive restaurant, with wine and candlelight—a real gentleman. Then he took me home in the limousine. But the minute he stepped inside my apartment, he changed. A real animal, this Izzy. Me, wearing my best dress, he ripped it off, threw me on the floor, and took me.

Sadie: Oy, I better break the date.

Rivkeh: No! Just wear a *shmatteh*.

77

A Jewish man, newly arrived from the Soviet Union, buys a car and begins driving happily all over Brooklyn. He is stopped by a policeman as he is driving down a one-way street in the wrong direction.

"You're going the wrong way," says the policeman.

The man looks at the policeman in amazement and says, "How did you know where I was going?"

78

You didn't think that was funny? It's not easy telling jokes to Jews.

You tell an Englishman a joke and ten minutes later he laughs.

You tell a Frenchman a joke and he smiles, parting his narrow mustache.

You tell a German a joke and he chortles—from the belly.

You tell a Russian a joke and he roars.

You tell a Jew a joke and he says, "I heard that one before."

79

The definition of a Jewish secret:
Something you tell only one person at a time.

80

Sign over a urinal in a bathroom at the Hebrew University:
"The future of the Jewish people is in your hands."

81

Two men are standing at the urinals in the San Francisco airport. One turns to the other and says, "You're from New York."

"Yes," says the other.

"Manhattan?"

"Indeed."

"On the West Side near Riverside Drive?"

"Yes. How did you know?"

"Between 82nd and 90th?"

"Extraordinary! But how do you know?"

"Well, the same *mohel* who cut you cut me; he cuts on a bias and you're pissing on my shoe."

Why is this joke so funny if told right? (The punchline has to be told quickly.) And it is funny. (A *mohel* is a ritual circumcisor, so now I can assume you understand the joke whether you think it's funny or not.) Actually, the joke makes no sense. It is one of those silly jokes. It is anatomically incorrect; there is no such thing as cutting (circumcising) on a bias; and it would not direct the flow of urine. So why is it so funny. In part because it is so ridiculous. In part because of the delay in the complaint.

82

After a visit to Hollywood, the Scottish director John Grierson is said to have remarked,

"After a few years in this place, your foreskin falls away."

83

The gentile wife to her husband:
"Buy Viagra."

The Jewish wife:
"Buy Pfizer."

84

Question: What does a Jewish wife make for dinner?

Answer: Reservations.

85

If you are in the middle of the forest, and your wife can't hear you, are you still wrong?

86

Two Jewish women are having lunch in a posh restaurant. Not long after their main dish has been served, the waiter returns and says,

"Is anything all right?"

87

Silly jokes are not for everyone. I love them. Here a few more.
The first one is a traditional story from the wise men of Chelm,
the town where everyone is ridiculous.

Two wise men of Chelm went out for a walk, when suddenly it began to rain.

"Quick," said one. "Open your umbrella."

"It won't help," said his friend. "My umbrella is full of holes."

"Then why did you bring it in the first place?"

"I didn't think it would rain!"

88

Katz is sitting naked in his room, wearing only a top hat, when Cohen walks in.

"Why are you sitting here naked?"

"It's all right," says Katz. "Nobody comes to visit."

"So why the hat?"

"Well, maybe somebody will come."

89

Abe and Sam are having a *glazzle tay* [a little glass of tea].
Abe stirs and stirs. "You know, Sam, life is like a glass of
tea."

"Why is life like a glass of tea?"

"So life isn't like a glass of tea."

Another version of the same joke:

"Life is like a glass of tea, Sam."

"You know, Abe, you're quite a philosopher."

90

Two *shlemiels* are kvetching about life. One of them sighs and says to the other, "Considering how hard life is, death isn't such a bad thing. In fact, I think sometimes it's better not to have been born at all."

"True," says his friend. "But how many people are that lucky? Maybe one in ten thousand!"

91

Life from a pig's viewpoint: Says one pig to another,
"Wouldn't it be a wonderful world if everyone were kosher?"

92

The phone rings in the law offices. A voice answers, "Zucker, Zucker, Zucker and Zucker."

"Hello, may I please speak to Mr. Zucker?"

"I'm sorry, but Mr. Zucker is in court."

"Well then, can I speak to Mr. Zucker?"

"Sorry, Mr. Zucker is with a client."

"Well, how about connecting me with Mr. Zucker?"

"Mr. Zucker is in Washington today."

Sigh. "O.K., then I'll speak to Mr. Zucker."

"Speaking."

93

Disc jockey Jack Spector was on the air one Yom Kippur when an indignant Jewish man telephoned him and demanded, "How can you, a nice Jewish boy, be working on Yom Kippur?"

"I'm not working," replied Spector, "I'm on tape."

This one has a hidden double whammy: What was the Jew doing listening to the radio and calling the disc jockey on Yom Kippur?

94

This one reaches back in time and is more traditional.

A poor Jew from Eastern Europe settles in a small town in the Midwest and almost disappears. He doesn't even have a name. He is known simply by his trade: *Schneider*, tailor. He barely ekes out a living for his wife and children. In desperation, he consults the rabbi, who tells him that he must take God as his partner.

So he does. He puts up a sign outside his shop, "*HaShem* and Schneider, partners."

Business improves and soon he is not only making a living, but he is thriving. He opens up a second store and then a chain of stores, each fancier than the last, each with a bigger sign than the last reading "*HaShem* and Schneider."

Finally, the time comes for the big move—to New York, to Manhattan, to Fifth Avenue! This is where he is going to make his mark in the world of haute couture. But as he is about to order the sign for the new store, he thinks to himself, "You know, that name was all right when I was a small timer, but now it has to be modernized, it has to fit Fifth Avenue. It has to be right for the world of high fashion."

But then he has second thoughts: "This was, after all, the name that made you successful."

Finally, he got it. Do what the immigrants always do when they come to America. Make it English. So that's what he did. He called it Lord and Taylor.

Even if you didn't know it before, you must have guessed what HaShem means. Literally, it means in Hebrew "the name;" observant Jews do not pronounce the name of God except in prayer. In ordinary conversation they simply refer to HaShem.

95

Here's a Hebrew double entendre:

King Arthur was reviewing his troops, all in a straight line, their armor gleaming—except for one. His armor was dull, even rusty, and falling apart. King Arthur was livid. He turned to his second in command and demanded to know: *"Mah nishtana ha-leilah ha-zeh?"**

*"Why is this night different from all other nights," the introduction to the famous four questions asked by the youngest child present at the Passover seder.

96

A cub reporter on an Israeli daily who has just made aliyah from America uncovers a great hot story that should get out right away. He comes running into the press room yelling, "Scoop, scoop! Stop the presses! Hold the back page!"

Hebrew, of course, reads from right to left, and Hebrew books go from—well, back to front.

97

Since we're now in Israel, let me tell you the secret of how to make a million dollars there:

Come with two.

It's not so true now. It's becoming very westernized and even prosperous. This is good for Israelis, but some of the jokes get dated. Like the next one. You can hardly imagine it if I were to substitute a modern prime minister for Ben-Gurion.

98

One evening Prime Minister Ben-Gurion was leaving his office for a formal UJA banquet in Jerusalem. An aide stopped him as he went out the door and said, "Mr. Prime Minister, you are going to a formal dinner. You can't go without a necktie and with your collar open like that."

"I can't?" asked Ben-Gurion. "Winston Churchill says this is all right, and you're going to tell me it's not?"

"Winston Churchill says it's all right?" asked the aide.

"Sure, he did," replied the Prime Minister. "Once, in London, I was going to a formal dinner party with him dressed like this, and he said, 'That kind of dress is all right in Israel, Mr. Prime Minister, but not in England.'"

A Texan is visiting a small town in northern Israel and in the market engages a Jew in conversation. After introducing himself, the Texan asks the Israeli what he does. "I raise chickens," the Israeli replies.

"Oh," says the Texan, "I'm a farmer, too. How much land do you have."

"Fifty meters in front, but almost a hundred meters out back."

"On my farm," says the Texan, "I can drive from sunrise to sunset and not reach the end of my property."

"That's too bad," says the Israeli, "I, too, had a car like that."

This is another joke about Israel. But you won't realize it until the punch line.

Melvin dies and has enough good deeds to his credit to give him a choice. First he takes the elevator up, where an angel shows him the virtues of heaven. Then he takes the elevator down—to hell. There he is greeted by the devil himself who leads him on an exciting tour of music, dancing girls, the finest food and special relaxing chairs. Melvin takes the elevator back up and ponders the situation for some time. Finally, he decides hell is the place for him. He packs his belongings in a suitcase, gets back on the elevator and presses the down button. Once again, he is met by the devil, but this time, the devil throws a shovel in his hand, the place is filled with fire and brimstone and Melvin is ordered to begin shoveling.

"What is this," Melvin asks, startled. "Before it was wine, women and song. Now this."

"Before you were a tourist," the devil replies. "Now you're an *oleh*."

An *oleh* is an immigrant to Israel. For many American Jews, it's one thing visiting Israel, but quite another living there.

101

An elderly Jew gets on the Greyhound Bus and sits down on a seat next to the window. On the seat beside him is a suitcase. He immediately opens his book of *Tehillim* (Psalms) and begins *davening* and *shockling*, back and forth mumbling the holy words in a sing-song monotone. The driver walks through the aisle and asks the man to put the suitcase on the rack above the seat. Unfazed, the man continues *shockling* and *davening*. On his next pass down the aisle, the driver gives the same instruction but a little more forcefully. Again the Jew ignores him, continuing to *daven* and *shockle*. On the third pass the driver shouts at him: "If you don't put that suitcase up on the rack," he says, "I'm going to throw it out of the bus."

Again ignored, the driver takes the suitcase and throws it off of the bus. The Jew continues to *daven* and *shockle*, except that in the same singsong monotone, he declares: "It vasn't even mine suitcase."

Acknowledgments

Behind every book there is someone who really does the work. In the case of this book it was Jodi Sperling who saw that my efforts were transformed into a manuscript and then into a book. The entire production process was supervised by Bridget Young. Both have my deep gratitude.

The daring cover, as well as the design of the interior, is the work of Rob Sugar of AURAS Design, whose creativity and judgment I have enjoyed now for over 20 years.

I am also indebted to friends, acquaintances and books for the jokes. I didn't make up a single joke in this book. In that sense nothing here is original. As a matter of fact, I don't know anyone who has actually made up a joke. Where do they come from? Someone must make them up. I don't even know from whom I heard most of the jokes in this book, so as to these I don't know whom to acknowledge. I do know where I heard or read some of these jokes, however, and I am happy to acknowledge with gratitude my indebtedness in those cases where I know it.

Hershel Shanks

Joke Credits

Bill Adler, *Jewish Wit and Wisdom* (New York: Dell Publishing, 1969).
9, 31b, 33, 93, 98

Lionel Blue on "Thought for the Day" Radio 4, (Monday, July 29, 1991)
15

Joseph E. Ellovich
26

Oded Eran
46

Steven Feldman
74

Eugene M. Grant
31

Joel S. Kaminsky
12

Alex Kozinski and Eugene Volokh, "Lawsuit, Shmawsuit," Yale Law
Journal, vol. 103, p. 463 (1993).
67

William Levine
59, 66

David Nimmer
4, 38, 94

William Novak and
Moshe Waldoks, *The Big Book of Jewish Humor*
(New York: Harper & Row, 1981).
21, 32, 35, 82, 87, 88

Larry Paul
19, 23,24, 34, 40, 41, 53, 56, 60, 63, 77

Jack Riemer
30

Meir Rosenne
16, 61a

Leo Rosten, *The Joys of Yiddish* (New York: McGraw-Hill, 1968).
5, 22, 32b, 36, 55, 73, 92

Julia Shanks
6, 76

Joseph Telushkin, *Jewish Humor: What the Best Jewish Jokes Say About
the Jews* (New York: William Morrow & Company, 1992).
7, 13, 14, 25B, 28, 42, 47, 51, 54a, 68, 80